To:

From:

Date:

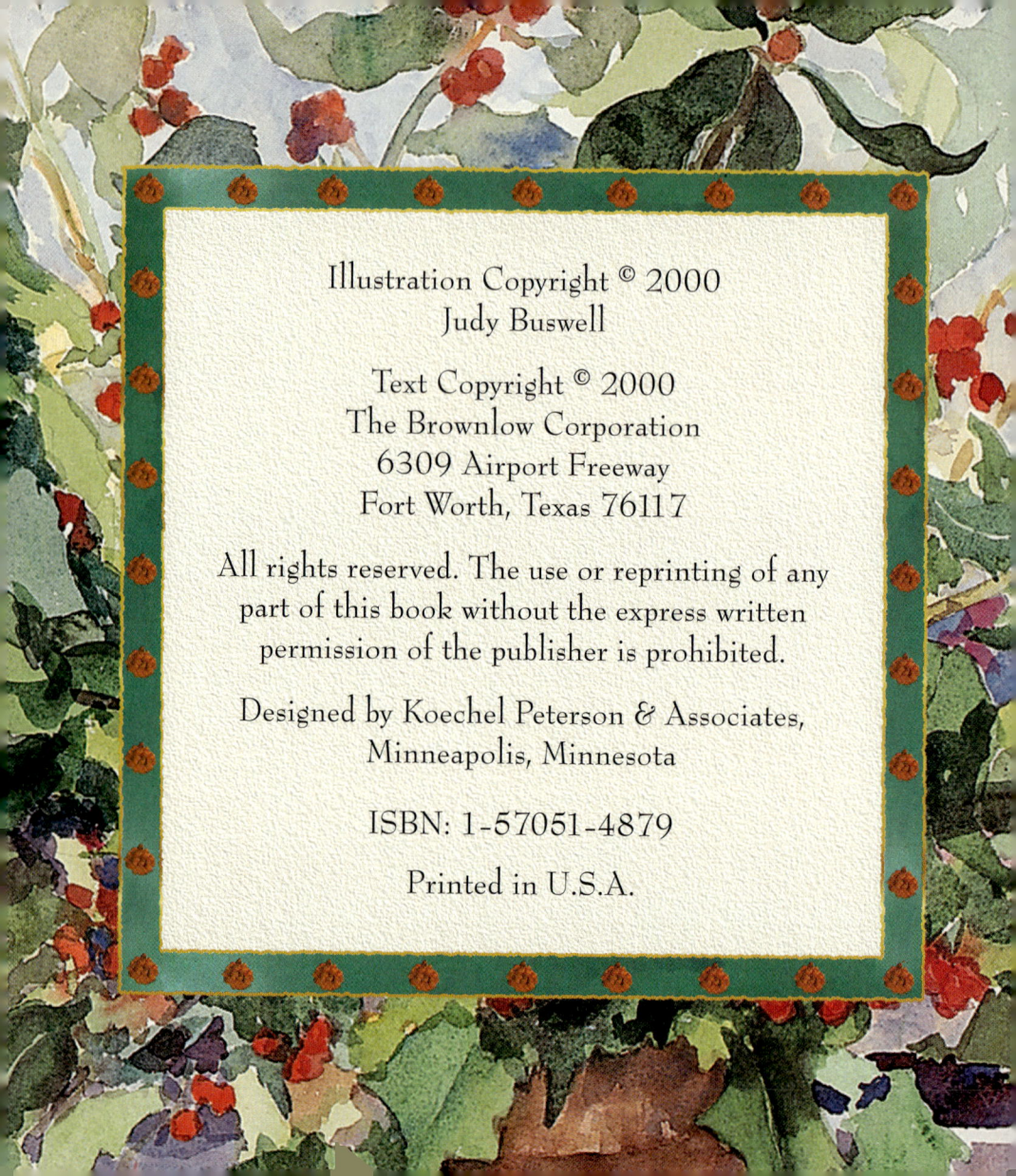

Illustration Copyright © 2000
Judy Buswell

Text Copyright © 2000
The Brownlow Corporation
6309 Airport Freeway
Fort Worth, Texas 76117

All rights reserved. The use or reprinting of any part of this book without the express written permission of the publisher is prohibited.

Designed by Koechel Peterson & Associates,
Minneapolis, Minnesota

ISBN: 1-57051-4879

Printed in U.S.A.

Home for the Holidays

A Fireside Collection to Warm the Heart

Illustrated by *Judy Buswell*

Written and Compiled by *Bonnie Jensen*

Foreword

Home for the Holidays is a collection of carefully selected quotes, poems, carols, Scriptures and stories that will invite your heart home for Christmas. Among the pages waiting to be penned with your own memories are gentle readings meant to warm you from the inside out. May this be a season full of memories and your favorite homegrown joys, and may this little book help to quietly take you there.

Home—Where Love Thrives

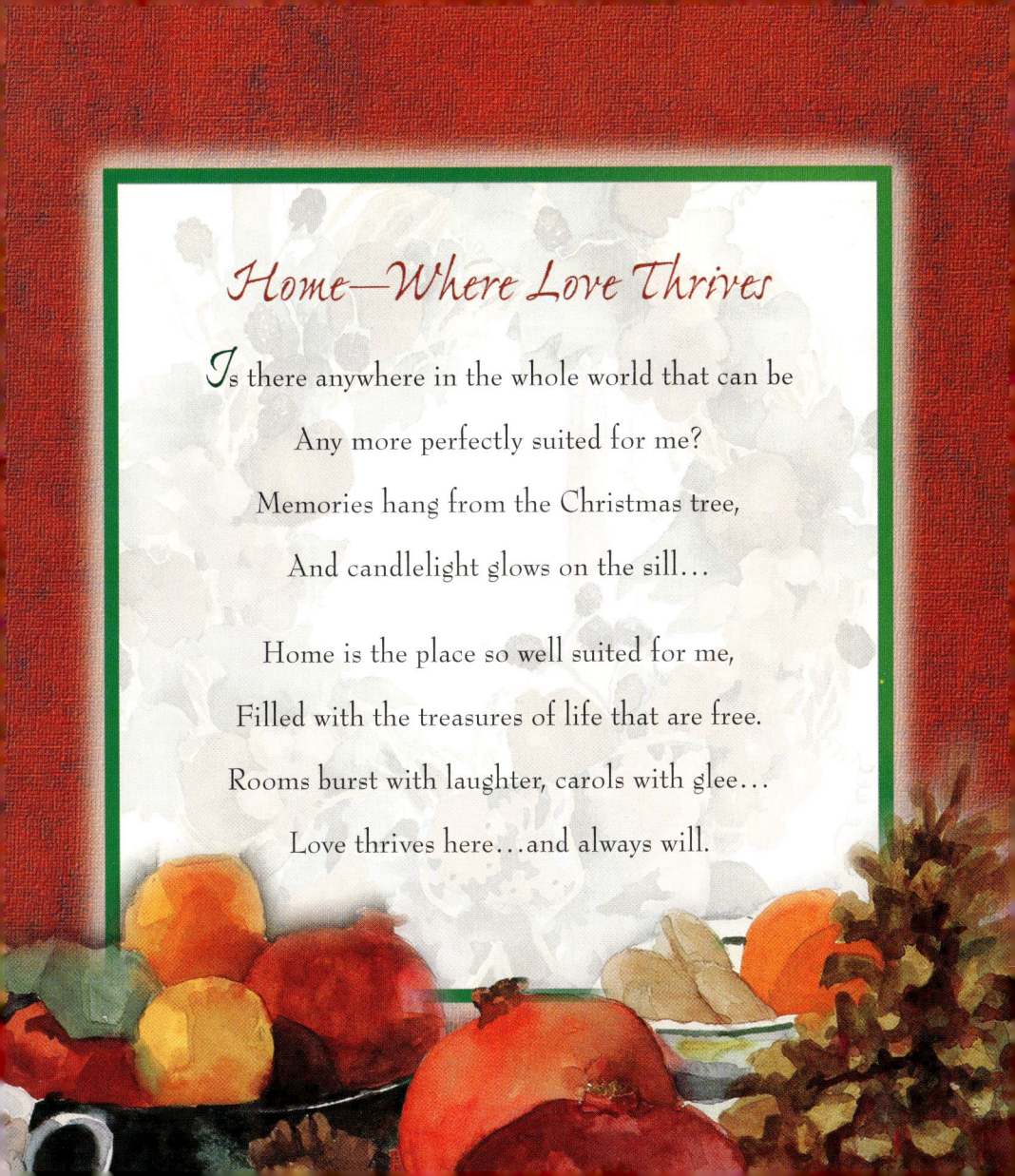

Is there anywhere in the whole world that can be

Any more perfectly suited for me?

Memories hang from the Christmas tree,

And candlelight glows on the sill…

Home is the place so well suited for me,

Filled with the treasures of life that are free.

Rooms burst with laughter, carols with glee…

Love thrives here…and always will.

A Christmas More Dear

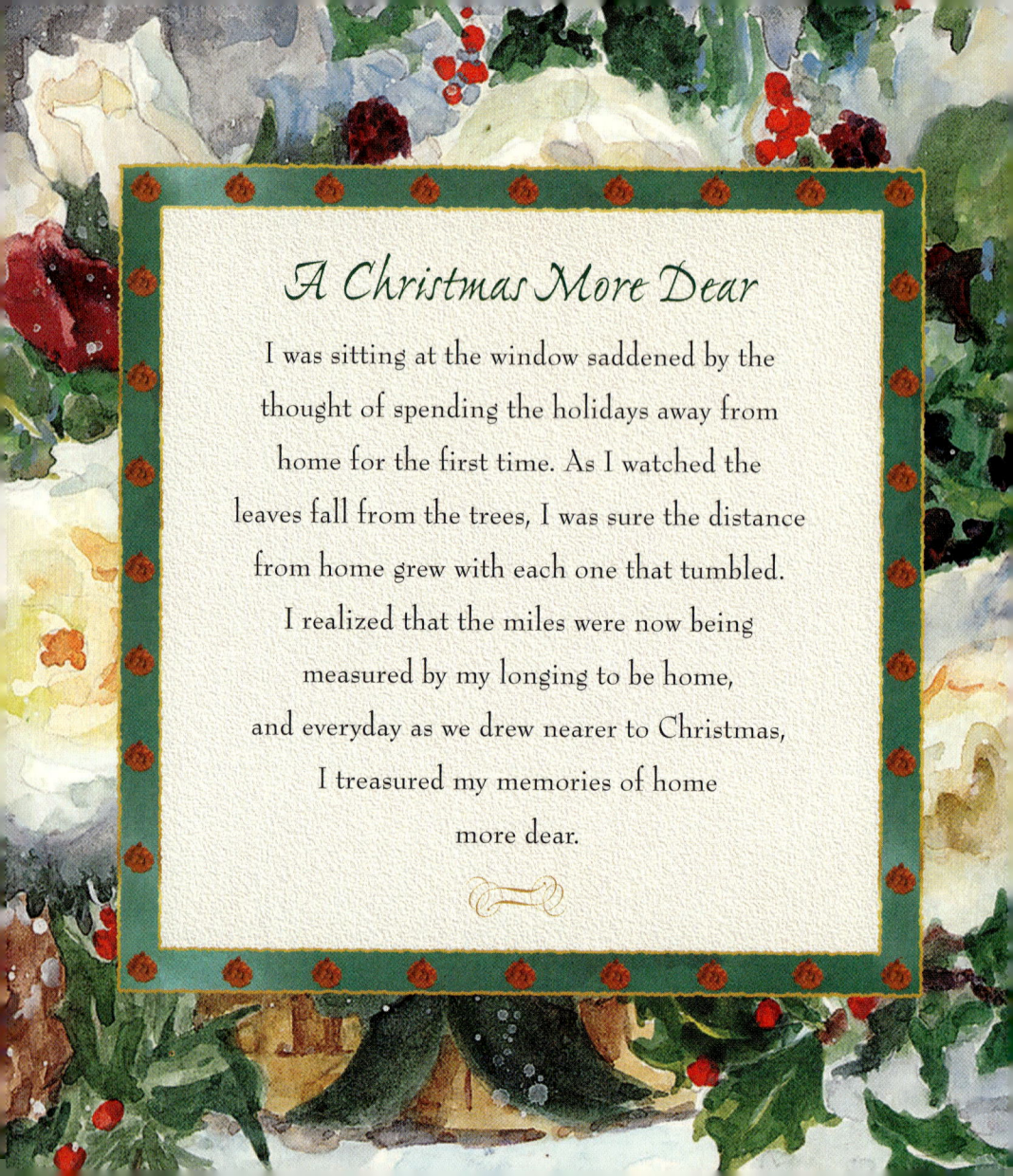

I was sitting at the window saddened by the
thought of spending the holidays away from
home for the first time. As I watched the
leaves fall from the trees, I was sure the distance
from home grew with each one that tumbled.
I realized that the miles were now being
measured by my longing to be home,
and everyday as we drew nearer to Christmas,
I treasured my memories of home
more dear.

Christmas Past
Memory Lane

Take a stroll, along with me,

and bring your favorite memory…

Grandma's Old-Fashioned Sour Cream Cut-outs

2 sticks butter
1 c. sugar
3 eggs
8 oz. sour cream
1 tsp. baking soda
1 tsp. baking powder
1 tsp. salt
5 c. flour
1 tsp. vanilla

Mix all ingredients in a large bowl and chill overnight.
Roll out (not too thin!) and use
your favorite Christmas cookie cutters.
Bake at 350 degrees for 6 to 8 minutes.
Let cool and top with Butter Frosting.

Butter Frosting

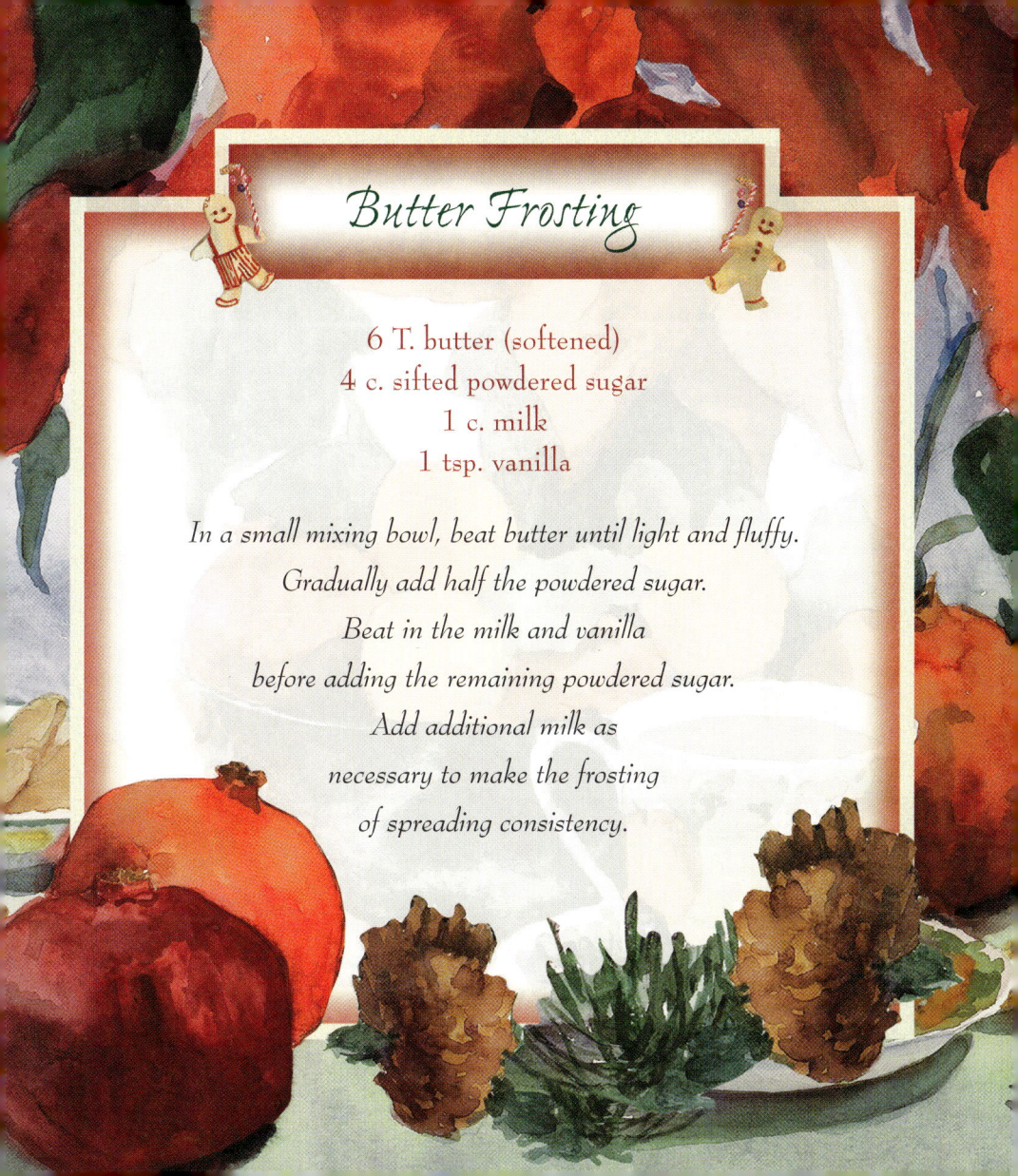

6 T. butter (softened)
4 c. sifted powdered sugar
1 c. milk
1 tsp. vanilla

In a small mixing bowl, beat butter until light and fluffy.
Gradually add half the powdered sugar.
Beat in the milk and vanilla
before adding the remaining powdered sugar.
Add additional milk as
necessary to make the frosting
of spreading consistency.

$\mathcal{A}$ gift that costs only time and a measure of kindness will outlive all others, for it will find a special place in the heart of the one who receives it.

*Those who give cheerfully give twice—
once to themselves and once to others*

—ANONYMOUS

...God loves a cheerful giver.

II CORINTHIANS 9:7

Priceless Gifts

A fun way to get your family into the spirit of giving during the Christmas season is to have each member devote themselves to giving "priceless" gifts just for a week or even a day during this wonderful time of year. "Priceless" gifts are ones that can't be purchased at a local mall or in your favorite store. Actually, they don't cost any money at all: a compliment, a helping hand, a note of appreciation. Children could give a hand-drawn picture or help in the kitchen even if it's not their turn.

The most important thing is that it doesn't have to be purchased. The blessing will be giving gifts that come from the heart; the reward will be learning that they are the very best gifts of all.

Joy to the World

Joy to the world!
The Lord is come:
Let earth receive her King.
Let ev'ry heart prepare Him room,
And heaven and nature sing,
And heaven and nature sing,
And heaven and heaven and nature sing.

PENNED BY ISAAC WATTS, 1719

And the angel said unto them, "Fear not: for, behold, I bring you good tidings of great joy, which shall be to all people. For unto you is born this day in the city of David a Saviour, which is Christ the Lord."

LUKE 2:10, 11

The Night Before Christmas

'Twas the night before Christmas
and all through the land,
Not a heart could conceive the
sweet birth God had planned.

The babe would not come here,
through castle or queen.
This heavenly child hailed
a kingdom unseen.

"Thou shalt call His name Jesus"
He'll save one and all,
In the name of the Father
each heart He will call.

Can you still hear Him beckon
with voice meek and mild...?
Simply listen...believe...
with the heart of a child.

A Single Toy, But Lots of Joy...

There's one particular childhood Christmas that stands out in my mind. It wasn't a tangible gift but a lesson learned that sustains the memory. My gifts that year were simple; an orange and a small wooden music box that played "Twinkle, Twinkle Little Star." I knew that soon after the gifts were opened we'd be on our way to my uncle's house in Florida, where we'd watch our cousins unwrap toy after glorious new toy.

The thought made me wish mom and dad didn't have to split their toy budget six ways—but I piled into our station wagon with my three brothers and two sisters for the annual holiday trek. As I sat squished in the seat, with laughter and excitement bouncing from one end of the car to the other, I soon forgot all about the gifts, caught up in the joy of the moment.

Later, with the maturity of years, I came to realize in some small way what the gifts of Christmas were—and they certainly couldn't be found under a tree. Toys come and go and last for only a season. But joy can last forever.

Christmas Candy Pizza

12 oz. semi-sweet chocolate chips

16 oz. white chocolate

Melt together semi-sweet chocolate with

14 oz. of the white chocolate (reserving 2 oz.).

Stir into the melted chocolate:

2 c. miniature marshmallows

1 c. rice krispies

1 c. peanuts

Pour into pizza pan and top with

1/3 c. coconut

and holiday colored M&M candies.

Finish by melting remaining

2 oz. of white chocolate

with 1 tsp. oil to drizzle on top of pizza.

Chill the candy until set, then simply break apart to

serve, or cut into thin "pizza slices".

Christmas Present
This Year's Bright Spots

Words are wonderful for preserving memories—
capturing details that time may fade.

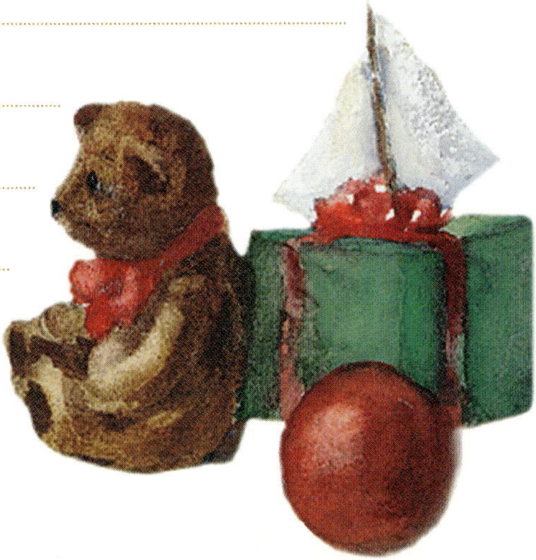

It was a snowy Christmas Eve in Oberndorf, Austria in the year 1818. Giant snowflakes fell like handcrafted ornaments from heaven. Joseph Mohr rubbed his forehead as he inspected the organ in his small village church. A mouse had chewed through the bellows making it impossible to play the organ for midnight service. "Dear, Lord," he whispered, "why would this happen on the very night our hearts are filled with praise for the miracle of Your birth?" Knowing the service wouldn't be complete without music, Joseph followed his quiet prayer with a humble attempt at songwriting. He needed one that could be learned quickly by the choir members and played on simple instruments. He passed the lyrics on to a schoolmaster who agreed to put them to music, and out of their last minute collaboration, the beloved Christmas song, "Silent Night," was born. When the beautiful melody fell upon the hearts of the villagers that night, Joseph knew his prayer had been answered... "Thank you, Lord, for the song you couldn't have given me without the timely intervention of a mouse."

Silent Night

Silent night, holy night!
All is calm, all is bright.
Round yon Virgin, Mother and Child.
Holy infant so tender and mild,
Sleep in heavenly peace,
Sleep in heavenly peace.

Silent night, holy night!
Shepherds quake at the sight.
Glories stream from heaven afar
Heavenly hosts sing Alleluia,
Christ the Saviour is born!
Christ the Saviour is born.

—*LYRICS*, JOSEPH MOHR
—*MELODY*, FRANZ GRUBER

Filled With Laughter

Can you laugh like a child again? It warms the room like nothing else in the whole wide world! The stove is filled with wood, the oven is warmed for dinner—but the preparations are not complete for Christmas if the rooms aren't filled up to the ceiling with pure, sweet laughter.

Peace on Earth

It came upon a midnight clear, that glorious song of old
From angels bending near the earth to touch their harps of gold
Peace on earth, goodwill to men, from heav'n's all gracious King
The world in solemn stillness lay to hear the angels sing.

EDMUND H. SEARS

And suddenly there was with the angel a multitude of the heavenly host praising God, and saying, "Glory to God in the highest, and on earth peace, good will toward men."

LUKE 2:13, 14

Lemon Snowdrops

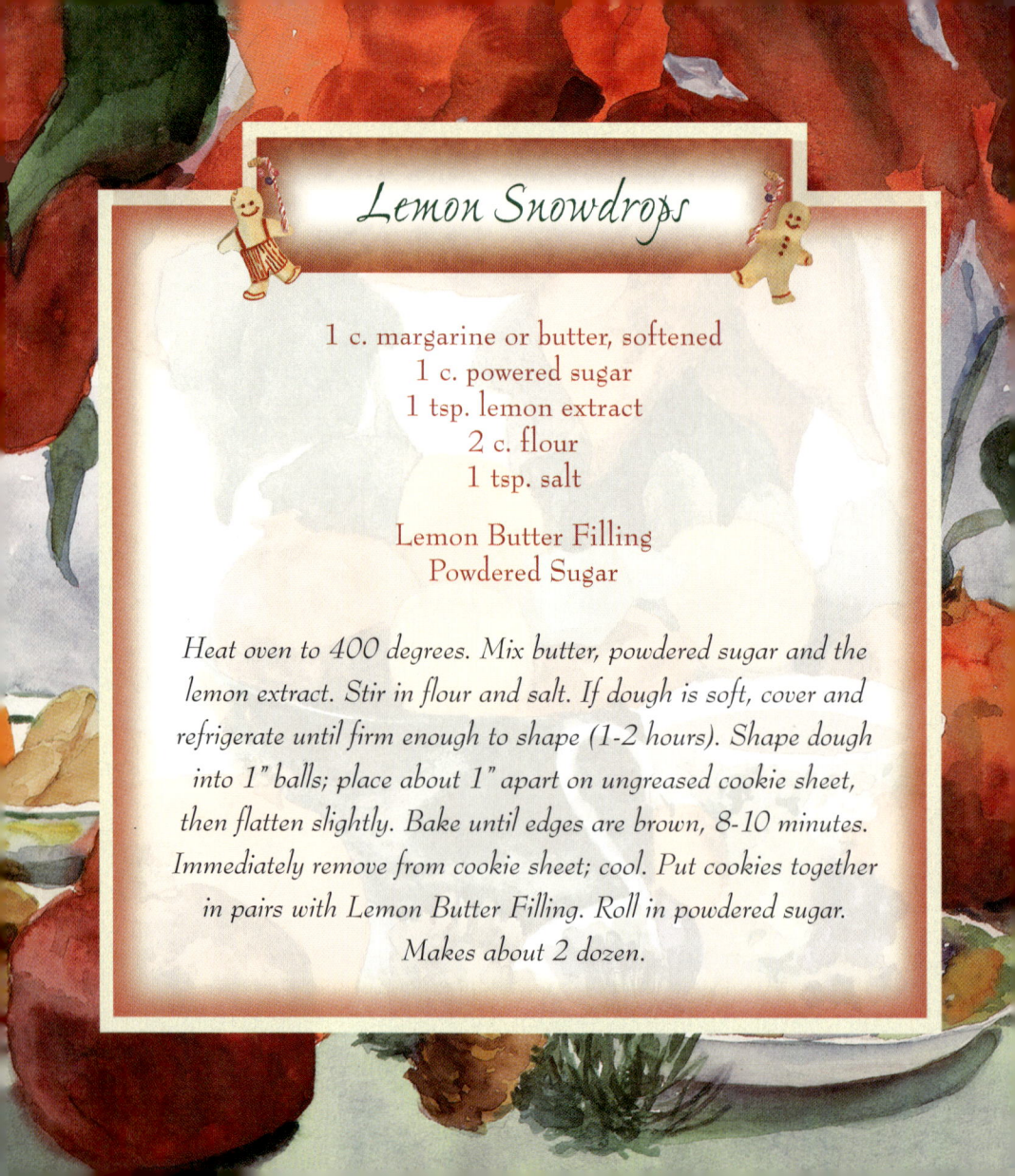

1 c. margarine or butter, softened
1 c. powered sugar
1 tsp. lemon extract
2 c. flour
1 tsp. salt

Lemon Butter Filling
Powdered Sugar

Heat oven to 400 degrees. Mix butter, powdered sugar and the lemon extract. Stir in flour and salt. If dough is soft, cover and refrigerate until firm enough to shape (1-2 hours). Shape dough into 1" balls; place about 1" apart on ungreased cookie sheet, then flatten slightly. Bake until edges are brown, 8-10 minutes. Immediately remove from cookie sheet; cool. Put cookies together in pairs with Lemon Butter Filling. Roll in powdered sugar. Makes about 2 dozen.

Lemon Butter Filling

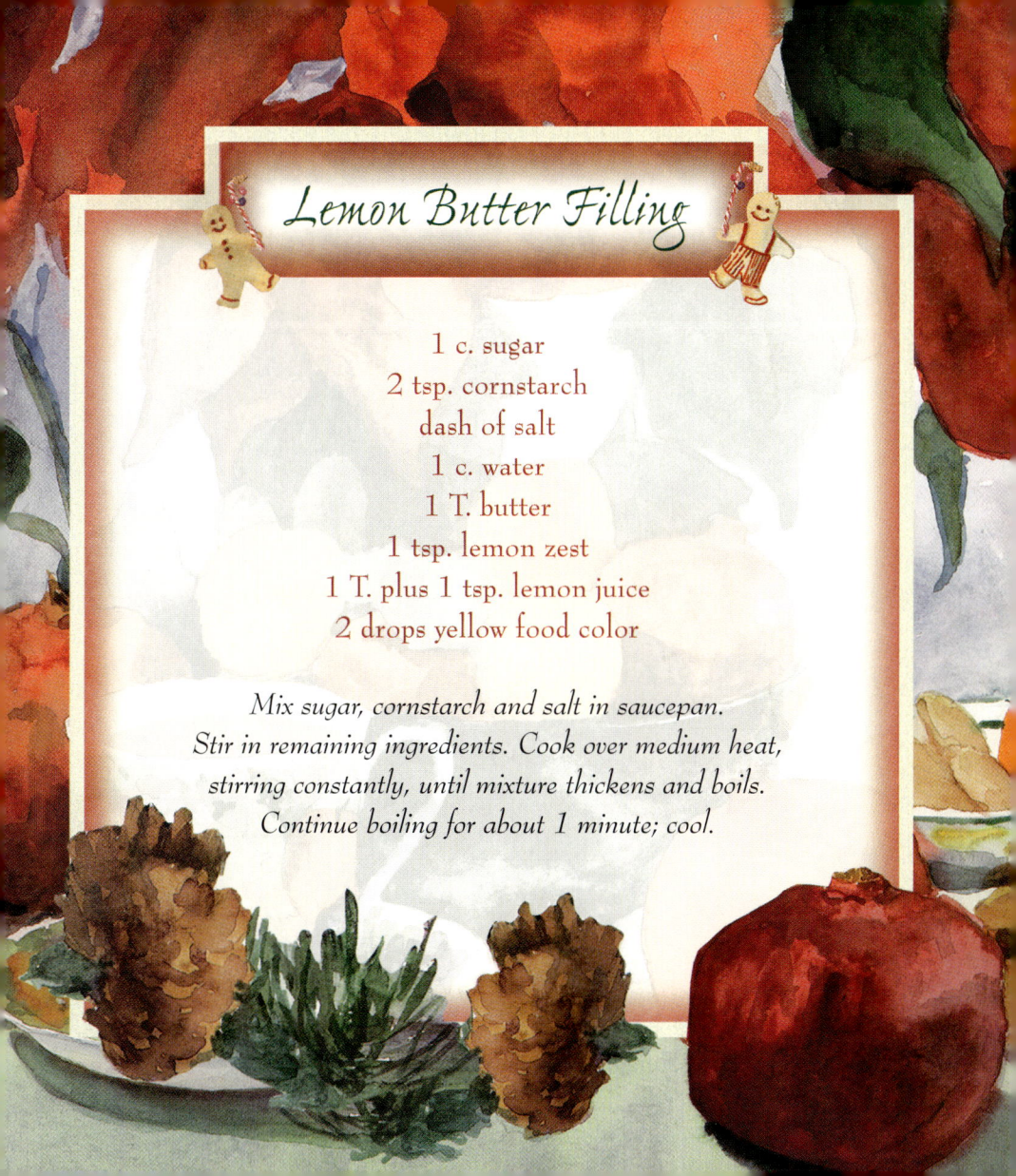

1 c. sugar
2 tsp. cornstarch
dash of salt
1 c. water
1 T. butter
1 tsp. lemon zest
1 T. plus 1 tsp. lemon juice
2 drops yellow food color

Mix sugar, cornstarch and salt in saucepan.
Stir in remaining ingredients. Cook over medium heat,
stirring constantly, until mixture thickens and boils.
Continue boiling for about 1 minute; cool.

Christmas On The Farm

Christmas Eve finally came and we could open presents. "Every available relative" (as Charles Dickens put it) was there, but no gifts could be opened before the "program." My cousins and I always had to sing Christmas carols, and the holly-jolly type like "Jingle Bells" just would not do. They wanted the old familiar religious carols of shepherds and sheep, Baby Jesus and the manger. One year we ended up singing the first verse of "Joy To The World" five times in a row because we couldn't remember the other verses, or any other song on the approved list. The presents were next, and while small, were most lovingly given and received.

Christmas morning began with the daily chores of feeding the animals and milking the cows. Once the farm was under control again, it was on to the last-minute preparations for Christmas dinner. At noon, all of us gathered for this final feast in the season of celebration. The well-fed but ill-fated turkey was there, along with ham from the smokehouse, mincemeat pies, and a dozen other things. I never really knew whether to believe my grandfather's tale of how he caught all those little "minces" for the pies, but I continue to perpetuate the story as gospel. I remember a lot about those times, but most of all I remember feeling safe, secure, and loved. Only now can I meagerly find the words to describe this season of abundance—an abundance of food, an abundance of family, an abundance of love.

PAUL C. BROWNLOW

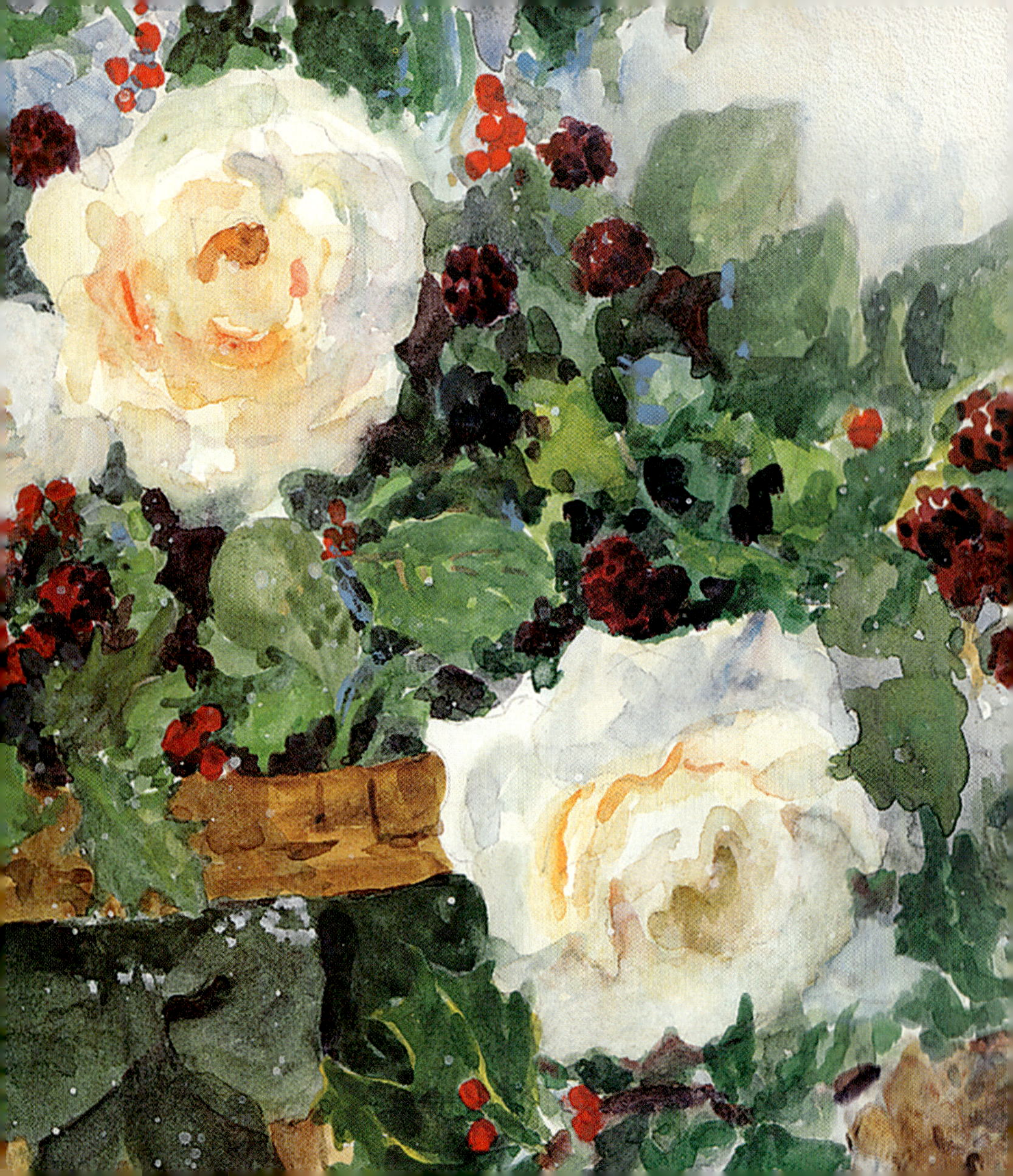

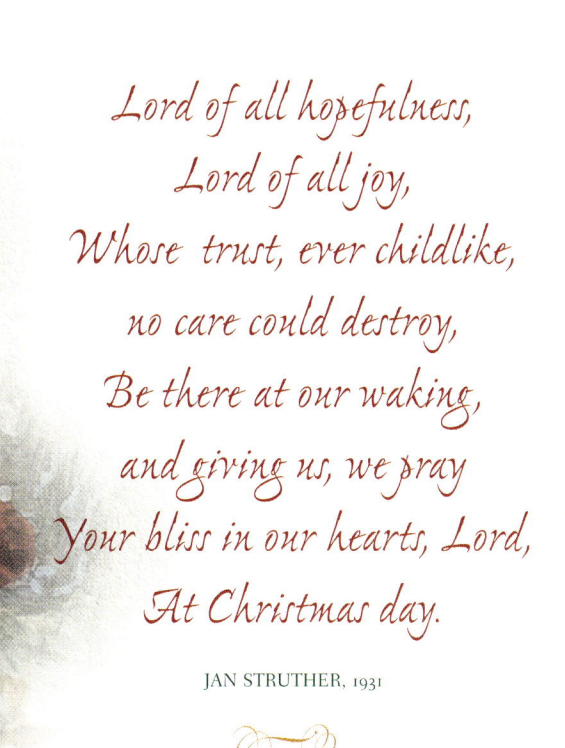

Lord of all hopefulness,
Lord of all joy,
Whose trust, ever childlike,
no care could destroy,
Be there at our waking,
and giving us, we pray
Your bliss in our hearts, Lord,
At Christmas day.

JAN STRUTHER, 1931

From quiet homes
and first beginning,
Out to the undiscovered ends,
There's nothing worth
the wear of winning,
But laughter
and the love of friends.

HILAIRE BELLOC, 1910

Our Guests This Christmas

O Christmas Tree

O Christmas Tree, O Christmas Tree,
With faithful leaves unchanging;
Not only green in summer's heat,
But also winter's snow and sleet,
O Christmas Tree, O Christmas Tree,
With faithful leaves unchanging.

O Christmas Tree, O Christmas Tree,
Of all the trees most lovely;
Each year, you bring to me delight
Gleaming in the Christmas night.
O Christmas Tree, O Christmas Tree,
Of all the trees most lovely.

TRADITIONAL GERMAN CAROL

Our Christmas Tree

In the Year of _____

PLACE
PHOTO
HERE

A Christmas Blanket

It is a giving God who could clothe the earth in
a luminous blanket of snow at Christmas time.
This He does so kindly in places least likely to be
washed in sunshine during winter's stay. The brightness
of a snow-covered ground gently rivals its celestial
light-bearer, and anyone who has squinted
in its brilliance will wholeheartedly agree.

*I'm dreaming of a White Christmas,
Just like the ones I used to know.*

IRVING BERLIN, 1942

Holiday Cheese Cups

3-8 oz. packages of cream cheese
5 eggs
1 c. sugar
1 tsp. vanilla
foil cupcake holders

Mix cream cheese until fluffy, then add other ingredients.
Fill cups full. Bake at 325 degrees for 25 minutes.
Remove from oven and let stand for 10 minutes.

Blend:
1 c. sour cream with 1 c. sugar
(add red or green food coloring)

Spoon this mixture into the
'valley' the cupcakes have developed.
Return to oven for 5 minutes. Makes 24 cheese cups.

Laughter and Song

I don't remember exactly when daddy started playing his guitar on Christmas Eve, but I know it's one of my favorite traditions to this day. From year to year he doesn't bother practicing our most beloved carols, he simply sits down by the fire on Christmas Eve and starts plucking out the first song that comes to mind. When he misses a note he smiles at all of us and continues strumming away with a look of pure joy in his eyes. I think he loves the challenge of trying to accommodate us, too, as we shout out song after song for him to 'play by ear'. It all seems fair in the end, as we stumble over as many words as he does chords, and it always turns into a priceless memory of laughter and song.

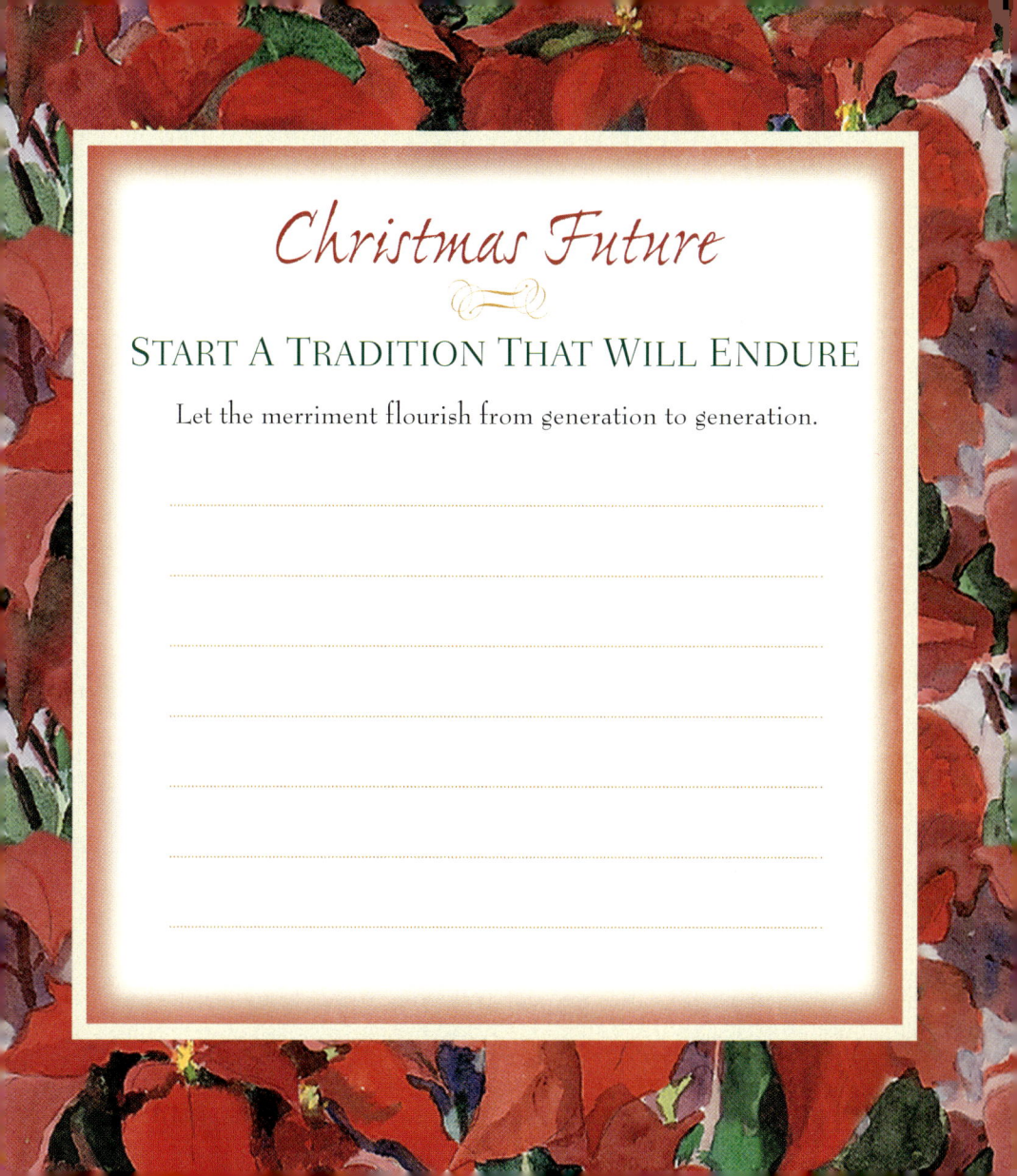

Christmas Future

Start A Tradition That Will Endure

Let the merriment flourish from generation to generation.

Do Something Special for Someone Special!

A handmade gift is always special because it is a personal expression of your love. Here are just a few handmade gift ideas to try.

God brings special people into our lives, many times to show us a glimpse of Himself.

ANONYMOUS

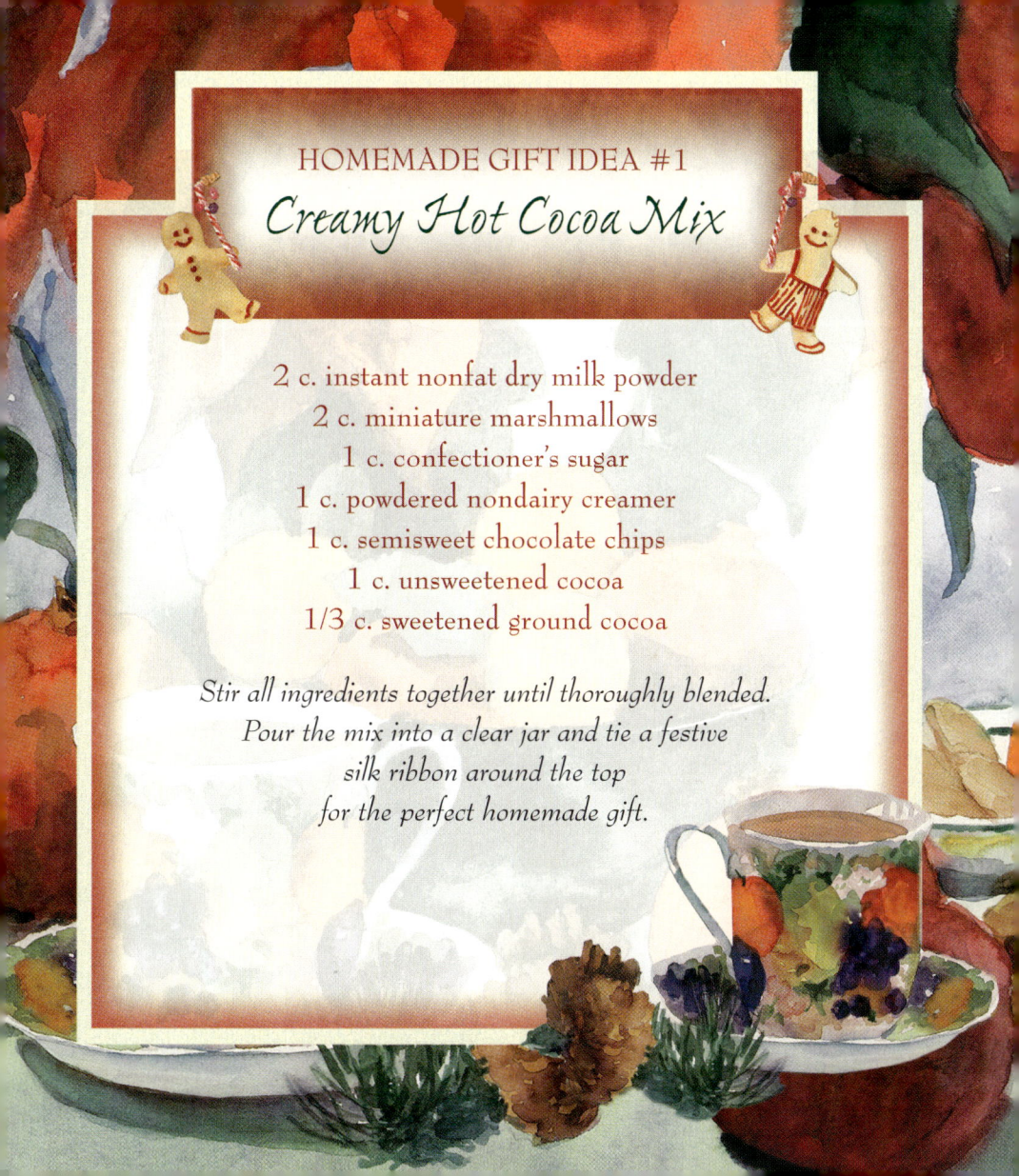

HOMEMADE GIFT IDEA #1
Creamy Hot Cocoa Mix

2 c. instant nonfat dry milk powder
2 c. miniature marshmallows
1 c. confectioner's sugar
1 c. powdered nondairy creamer
1 c. semisweet chocolate chips
1 c. unsweetened cocoa
1/3 c. sweetened ground cocoa

*Stir all ingredients together until thoroughly blended.
Pour the mix into a clear jar and tie a festive
silk ribbon around the top
for the perfect homemade gift.*

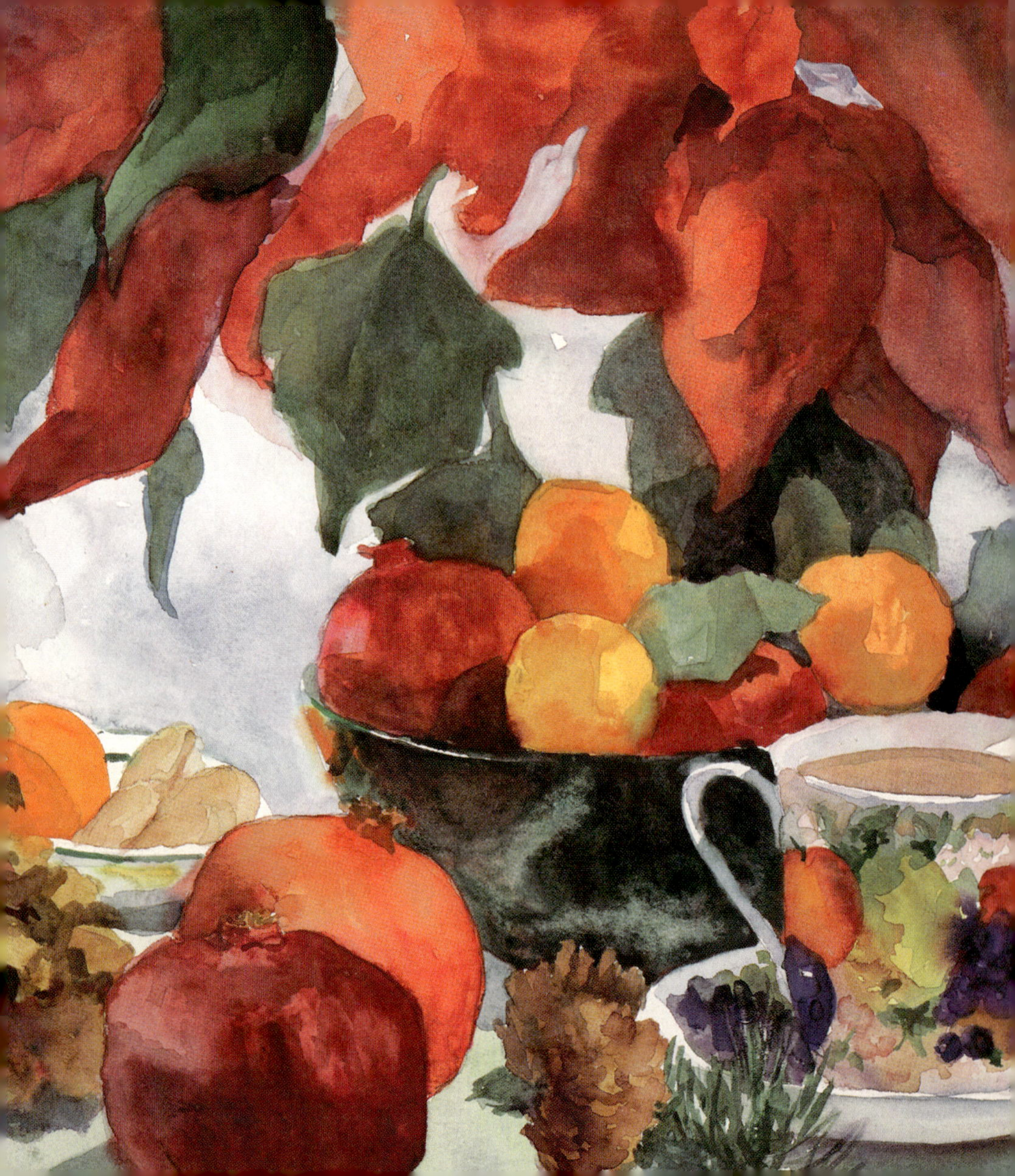

HOMEMADE GIFT IDEA #2
Decadent Homemade Hot Fudge

1 c. sugar
1 c. heavy cream
1 c. light corn syrup
6 T. butter
pinch of salt
1 tsp. vanilla
1-1/2 c. quality brand unsweetened cocoa

Stir together butter and sugar over medium heat until butter melts. Add remaining ingredients—cocoa last. Boil for 2 minutes, stirring constantly. Let sauce cool down a bit before filling approximately two decorative quart jars. Make festive labels for the jars and tie a ribbon around the top. Seal tightly and refrigerate until gift giving time!

*Merry Christmas to all...
and to all a good night.*